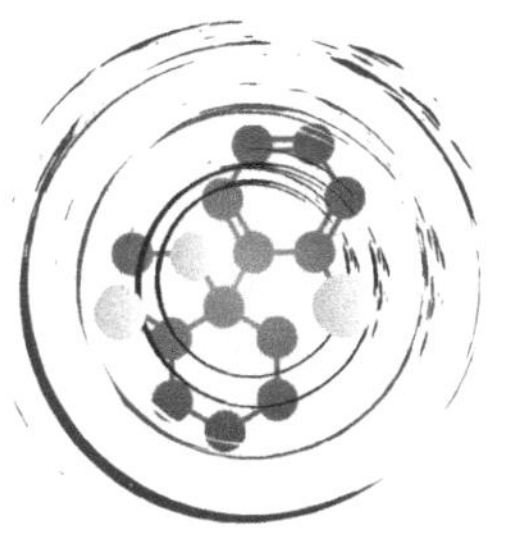

SHUT UP EGO

*A Ketamine
Trip Report*

Anthony Farina
with Robbie Grayson III

ATTRIBUTIONS
Interior Text Font: Minion Pro
Cover Design & Typesetting: Robbie W, Grayson III
Additional Credits on Credits Page

ISBN:

BOOK PUBLISHER INFORMATION
Traitmarker Books
A Division of Traitmarker Media
www.traitmarkerbooks.com
traitmarker@gmail.com

Table of Contents

A Note from the Publisher

The publisher is providing this book and its contents on an "as is" basis and makes no representations or warranties of any kind with respect to this book or its contents and disclaim all such representations and warranties, including but not limited to warranties of mental healthcare for a particular purpose.

The content of this book is for informational purposes only and is not intended to diagnose, treat, cure, or prevent any mental/social condition or disease. This book is not intended as a substitute for consultation with a licensed practitioner. Please consult with a physician or healthcare specialist regarding the suggestions and recommendations made in this book.

The Purpose of This Little Book

In the summer of 2021, I was in my apartment where my best friend—my Bernese Mountain Dog named Ambush whom I had with me for nearly ten years—passed away. I had also just ended some long-term friendships, so I needed to be in a better place than I was.

I decided to go on a trip that night, so I took two handfuls of indica and made a small French tea press. I drank the whole French press in thirty minutes, demanding to know from whatever god was listening what was wrong with me and what I needed to do. As odd as it might sound, this part is what set me on my journey to find healing. The trip that night ended hellish in a beautiful way if you can believe me.

I went to lie down after I finished my tea, thinking I screwed something up because I felt nothing. As I lay down, I felt hands on my back: little baby koala angel hands is how I describe it. I was feeling bliss. And then a voice in my head spoke.

"Do not roll over on your left side."

I laughed. And instead of heeding the warning, I rolled over. Immediately, I felt like the room had shifted and thrown me to the other end. Yet I was still in my bed.

Throughout the night, I thought I had lived in my apartment for 10,000 years and that my reality was all fake. It was one of the scariest situations I have ever endured, only second to the first time I was shot at in combat.

Toward the end of my trip, I wanted nothing more than to escape the madness from hours of living in a distorted reality.

Then it hit me. I kept hearing these voices saying I was going to die. After some time, I remembered what Joe Rogan had said about what to do if you are in a bad trip.

"You just gotta let go."

So I did. I just let whatever was going to happen take its course. The next moment, the madness stopped and I heard something in my mind speak to me.

In the end, you don't even own you.

Suddenly, things got really bright. I woke up late the following day feeling grateful. It was this "trip" incident that set me on my journey to find out why psychedelics have this power and what I could take in a controlled setting that would prove beneficial. Ketamine was the answer, and here is my experience.

Anthony Farina
Statersville, Rhode Island | January 2024

Anxiety is love's greatest killer. It makes others feel as you might when a drowning man holds on to you. You want to save him, but you know he will strangle you with his panic.

ANAIS NIN

trip 1

A few years ago, I moved from Indiana to Utah and found a company called Mindbloom that offered ketamine therapy. You can also get IV therapy at a doctor's office, but doing this in my home was more appealing. I was approved for treatment and would be given one dose a week, delivered to my door, and then I would talk to a doctor before my session of taking the pill.

I put the ketamine pill in my mouth and held it under my tongue as instructed. I was told not to spit for seven minutes. During that time, the onset was rapid. Within sixteen seconds, the full-blown god-awful taste was unbearable.

After about a minute and a half, I felt this wave of calmness. About five minutes in, I felt slightly off-balance and wanted to lie down. By the time seven minutes arrived, I spit the pill out and quickly lay down. My sitter had to help me get situated and even started my playlist for me. I put my earbuds in, put the eye mask on, lay back, and tucked in. The journey began.

My senses began to adjust to the combination of darkness and pleasant music, increasing my sense of smell. A moment later, my eyes felt like they wanted to move back and forth, mimicking rapid eye movement just like EMDR: an effective therapy I underwent nearly three years ago. Rapid eye movement is key in connecting neurons between the two hemispheres in the brain to bridge the analytical side with the emotional and creative side, helping to reach catharsis with past traumatic memories and issues.

I then began to want to laugh but noticed my body and spirit doing something weird. My physical body was lying on the bed while my spirit was being pulled off to my left.

Before long, I reached a place of total and absolute love. I immediately recognized this place as home. My real home. I was able to interpret what real love was. I felt ecstasy, euphoria, joy, happiness, fulfillment, and many other emotions that are watered down when compared to the total encompassing feeling of what love really is.

This place was a field surrounded by trees and bright light. I didn't see anyone right away, but I knew others were present at that exact moment in this dimension. I understood love to its fullest and realized when we chase a lust, a drug for relief, or anything like that, we are putting effort into going after a minor fractional byproduct of what really constitutes true and complete love.

The love I felt in my true home really is hard to explain. It was a sense of completeness, knowing I was where I came from and wanting to stay. I was safe and felt like I had been gone for a very long time. I also knew this home was always with me from the start of my physical life. It's been right inside me. I just didn't know how to access it.

You don't need to ask questions in this place because what you want to know is made known instantly. I was immediately made aware that I am loved very much by many people. Too often, I feel someone doesn't really love me, which makes me feel lonely. False beliefs often became more prevalent in my relationships as I began to doubt those who have tried to show me love. It's not that I am unloved. It's that I chose to believe I wasn't worthy of love from others.

MADE WITH LOVE
MADE WITH LOVE

A wave came over me, which was my first epiphany of this experience. I realized that it was so simple to understand that we are loved dearly by many people on and off this earth. It is such a simple and easy truth that we make more difficult than it really is in this life.

I saw a friend and was shocked. He died long ago in the war. I had watched him die. I even asked, *What are you doing here? You're dead. I watched you die.*

He just smiled, and something told me he wanted to say, *You will get it soon enough. We will all come back here, and we will see each other another time.*

I told him he was a good kid and did his job well. He laughed and said, *Who is the kid exactly?*

After this, I went to another place where I saw the circular, wavy, black outline of a figure. The inside of this figure was a yellow light. It changed in shape and then faded out of my understanding. Then, a set of words came to me, and I knew I needed to remember them.

The reason for all of existence is love.

It sounds so cliché' and simplistic, but as I learned later, this phrase has much more depth.

I was then shown more of who I was and why I am here.

I understood that I am a being who is meant to love deeply. My job in this life is when I come across anyone (and given the opportunity) I am to reach into their heart, pull out the love within them, and show it to them. That way, no matter what troubles and heartache anyone is enduring, I can show them that through all that pain, there is an immense amount of love deep within their soul.

This is an important job I have been given in this life because there is so much pain, despair, cruelty, and hatred in our world and way of life. Too often, we not only give up on the idea of being loved, but we fail to see that it is always inside us.

My purpose, then, is to reach as many people as possible in the 84 years I will have in this life and to show them the love they hold inside. By doing this, I help love continue throughout all of existence.

Each of us has a job that in some way is about spreading love. There is one single infinitely grand-in-size source of love at the center of and through our existence. Each of us knows our tasks to ensure that love continues. If all of us were to stop doing this, then darkness would consume everything. It would overrun the light, suffocating any outlets for love to continue through.

I watched next as I was shown that I had put on a suit, like a space suit, before coming here. This is because my work involves being exposed to painful emotions and events. The suit protects my true nature and source of love, thus letting me continue my work, absorbing the negativity of others.

Sometimes, the suit can get so heavy that I get distracted from my purpose. In the past, I would turn to drink, drugs, or women to feel good—to find a little escape from the weight of the suit. Keeping your suit light is key to operating efficiently.

Darkness fights against the light. The light receives its source from love. *Love is the source.* The floating yellow mass with dark edges reappeared when I realized this last part. This time, I was drawn to it and wanted to go straight for the center. It faded the more I understood the current lesson.

Next, I was in darkness, and the face of a rat, cow, or wolf appeared. It was hard to make out, but it could have been more friendly. It had a long snout with grey and green eyes. It didn't just appear. It slowly came into the picture. I didn't get a good vibe, but I knew it was showing itself to me for a reason. I spoke to it, asking what it was. It was something dark and born of trauma.

I asked what I needed to learn from it and what it could teach me. I'm not sure if it was because I didn't show fear but wanted to learn from it, which is what made it retreat into the darkness, but it did. As it faded slowly, I stopped and looked at myself. I told it I would see it again but to know that I accepted whatever it is. It disappeared for good.

The yellow floating mass appeared again and grew bigger. I'm more drawn to it now. Then it faded, and I found myself drifting, going into nowhere. For some reason, I wanted to see If I was totally disconnected from my body or what was going on. I decided to move my right hand, and I did so instantly. I realized I did, and the funny thing was that as soon as I realized I had control over my physical body while still being in this other place, I remember saying to myself, *Well, that is fucking boring. I'm going to jump back into the void.*

And away I went.

What occurred next was that I began asking a bunch of questions. As soon as I asked, I would get an answer. I don't know what they were, but even as I type this, I can tell that those answers are within me and I feel reassured that I have all I need to know in this life.

Things started to end. I was in some place, standing on a platform. All around was light, and there were others. Everyone was a blue transparent being, all in perfect form. I recognized some people I know here in this life who have been with me for a very long time. I had happy and relieved memories with those loved ones in a fraction of a second.

The next moment, I was standing on the edge of this platform with several others who are family and friends. We were all looking down at where we would go. As we stepped off the platform, we would become an energy-shaped cone with the tip pointed down toward Earth.

Before this happened, I asked what the point of this was because I was pretty sad. I had just arrived and was already saying goodbye again to loved ones. I was made aware that we all will find each other in the coming life and will part again through death. We will meet again at home, learn what we must do, and prepare to return—repeating the cycle of dying in the ethereal life, only to be born again in corporeal form.

I was more upset with this answer and wanted to know why we couldn't all be together. Why do we have to keep saying goodbye to one another over and over again? Everything faded instantly, and I was shown the totality of darkness. I was made to know that our job is to keep love alive in all ways possible, and as we do so, all of our existence will continue.

Each act of love that is shown pierces the darkness. It isn't a matter of wanting to stay in the ethereal realm because we all are glad to make this journey. We do this because it is our duty. Also, because we are beings of love. Not living an existence based on love will create an existence without meaning. The consequence is that if our acts of love die, then we all die. Everything in every universe where there is light will die.

At this moment, I was absorbed into the fabric of emptiness: the deep, infinite void of nothing in order to understand the depth of darkness. Even at this point, I felt I was not alone. I was being shown what the absence of love truly is.

That absence on a small scale is what we feel when a loved one dies. When we suffer heartbreak. When we hurt those we love from our selfish nature. We must all fight against the darkness because it fights to consume love. And you come from love incarnate.

After the First Dose

I spoke with a good friend who was in a coma for 30 hours. He read my trip report and was shocked at how much he could relate. He also felt that he received some answers and a bit of closure.

He also mentioned his sense of smell: how he smelled his body burning. After some discussion, we learned that the sense of smell is the second-to-the-last sense to go before you die, followed by hearing.

The issue I am plagued with now is that I got a taste of what home was like—the joy, beauty, and happiness that culminated into such bliss that you had no choice but to realize love flows through everything. And I *do* mean *everything.* Since I got that taste of home, things here just seem dull. I realize there is no reason for more than half the problems in my life.

Binding up my intentions with wasted things and ruminating all the time has eroded the quality of my life. Everything at home was complete, happy, and how it should be. The only thing I felt got in the way was when I was in that place was a feeling of longing.

I wanted to share this beauty with others at home but couldn't. There is nothing on this earth that can compare to the sort of bliss you will experience when you are home. When the time comes after death and everyone you know has crossed over, that longing will be gone and you can enjoy that eternal happiness.

Except it's not eternal: you die an ethereal death only to return to a corporeal life. I will say that I will stay home a little longer this time. I'm tired.

GAME
OVER

The Day After

Effects are felt after a good night's sleep. For months, I had not been able to sleep more than five to six hours a night. I was constantly waking up tired and in a bad mood.

The first night after I took ketamine, I slept about seven hours. The following night was a little over eight. And last night, I slept ten hours and woke up feeling great. I have vivid dreams that reflect current situations in my life, and these dreams are helping me to untangle things in my subconscious.

Last night's dream was about letting go of the things dragging me down. I was in front of a mirror and saw part of myself and then part of another person I knew. I realized I had been deflecting my good qualities onto others, giving away my power. I woke up feeling like I could take charge of my life by reclaiming my energy again.

The mental effect is that I feel grounded in who I am and who I will become in the near future. The words we speak to ourselves and others are not mere words. *They are spells.* And if we put intention and belief behind those words, things will change in your favor.

One issue still plagued me: the guilt I felt about not wanting to be here in this life. This is not associated with suicidal thoughts or depression. This feeling is where you know there is a much better place than your current place. The longing I felt for what I now call my true home still consumes me to this day. It's a happy feeling because I know that ultimate joy exists, and I will be in that place again.

But the happiness is also mixed with a touch of disappointment as I bring myself back to my current reality, understanding the true work to be done in this life. And I cannot leave this life until that job is done—mastering the art which is your life.

*The punishment of
every disordered mind
is its own disorder."*

St. Augustine of Hippo

trip 2

The second trip was uneventful. The sitter wasn't really great. I ate and drank too close to taking the medicine. And I didn't meditate or focus on what I wanted.

I also broke a cardinal rule: I let expectations be the dominant thought of my mind as I went under. You are not supposed to focus on thinking that a specific thing will happen. You are supposed to relax and let your mind go blank. All your thoughts are to race through your mind as if they were simply passing through.

Instead, I kept grasping particular thoughts and dwelling on them, which made it hard to clear my mind.

The message of this trip was oneness. I was faced with two versions of myself and understood that these versions are always present. It is a matter of which version I choose to feed during any given micro-action or choice in my daily life. The one you feed more is the one that becomes more dominant.

If you feed the wrong version of yourself long enough and decide later on that you want to change for the better, the version you were feeding will often retaliate in the form of regret and negative emotions. This was my ego, the version I had let dominate my choices when I should have made the decision to silence it.

I was then shown myself from the third person's point of view. I was ready for this lesson, and it was about controlling urges. But as I felt ready to receive the lesson, the trip ended abruptly.

I didn't get much introspection from this trip and noticed things more on the physical side than the introspective one. So, there is not much to report. I was told this is common for the second trip because of how grandiose the first trip can be.

The one issue, however, was my sitter during this session. I mention this because of how important it is to choose a good sitter. She was not a good one from the beginning. She was less familiar with performing duties, so there was less trust from the start. I don't like to focus just on the negative, so the real value of this trip was finding out what to avoid and what to focus on during future trips.

This played a big role in the overall success of this experience with ketamine. I would come to find out that ketamine was working in my brain around the clock, as the doctor had stated it would. Once you take a dose of ketamine, it continues to work for days afterward.

After this session, I got some sleep, On the next day, I began to take note of certain things that were happening in my life: mainly how my addictions, depression, and anxiety were decreasing. Out of eight addictions before my first treatment, I noticed a decrease in the cravings.

Using a scale of 1 to 10 with a 10 for feeling depressed every day to the point of losing one's purpose, I would rate that my depression decreased from 8/10 to 6/10.

My anxiety decreased the most, going from a daily 7/10 to a 5/10. I noticed I wasn't thinking as much about all the bad things that could play out in my future. Anytime I would start to think of something playing out badly and notice my heart rate spike, a comforting feeling would come over me and I would ask why I was thinking this way and what evidence there was that it could happen.

Six months before my first dose, I underwent surgery on my foot, which was still in pain every day and in need for another major surgery. But what I noticed was that the pain wasn't as bad on that day as in previous days.

I was taking two 800mg Motrin and 2000mg Tylenol rapid release twice a day. For two weeks, I stopped taking Motrin entirely and reduced my Tylenol intake to 2000mg once a day. I remember reading that Ketamine isn't a pain reliever, so this made me question what was going on.

I wondered if this is why I was taking less Tylenol and Motrin and why I have been quickly stopping my addictions. Not because Ketamine was blocking pain receptors but because it was making me forget I had pain in my foot.

After my first session, I was walking around the house and opened a drawer in my kitchen where I put my medications. I found a hydrocodone and felt the urge to take it, but the urge quickly subsided, which caught me off guard. I then remembered that in preparation for my first Ketamine session, I stopped taking painkillers three days before, getting it out of my system.

When I opened the kitchen drawer, it would have been a little over a week since I had taken my last dose. If my understanding is correct, Ketamine helped me forget that I needed something like this, thus helping me to stop taking it.

Differences Between Trip 1 & 2

More addictions were curbed. Less anxiety, less depression. I was working out with a clearer mind. Sleep quality has significantly improved. The feeling of wanting to be connected to my local community was new, and I haven't felt that in over ten years.

I was again faced with the third-person view, the fly on the wall. It was a memory of another person and me arguing. I was feeling everything that I felt during that argument. Then the argument stopped. I watched the argument play out again, but I felt everything the other person felt this time. I understood that they were mainly reacting to how I was being.

The argument stopped and replayed a final time where I felt neither my emotions nor the other person's. I was witnessing what it would look like from a stranger watching. I felt embarrassed and ashamed. What's interesting is that later I would hear a story about how Buddha went to a town. While talking to the townspeople, a man in the back of the crowd kept shouting obscenities at Buddha, trying to attract the holy man with all his might. After Buddha had finished talking to the crowd, he began to walk away from the town. The man quickly caught up to Buddha and asked him why he didn't react to his slurs.

"When you give someone a gift," Buddha asked, "who has the choice to accept it?" The man replied, "The person I gave it to." Buddha responded, "That is the same with negative emotions. If someone tries to give me their anger, and I do not accept it, who ends up keeping it?" The man realized the errors of his ways. And so did I.

trip 3

Stop associating with low-level shit. Our life journey is like climbing from one platform to another. When we are on one level of the platform, above us is another, but chains, wires, or something else hang from that platform. To climb up to the next platform, we must remove the obstacles on the current platform.

The obstacles are not there to make our lives hard or punish us. They are there to teach us what we need to know to endure the hardships in life and become the best version of our current selves.

trip 4

I found my inner child inside a metal room. It was empty, and I was curled up in the corner of the room, squatting, tired, alone, and afraid. But confidence comes from being true to ourselves.

During my childhood, I went through a lot of pain, but all I needed was imagination, my friends, and family. I did not need wealth or fame.

The light comes from within the darkness and consumes it. If you feel you are in total darkness, it is likely because of that point in your life. If you are the *only* light in the darkness, it is no wonder you cannot see other lights.

We need to take inventory of what we are grateful for. By doing so, we can make the most use of what we already have, bringing us to the most efficient point of happiness.

Our wants are the true illusion. When we set our sights on something we want, we forgo making what we have a part of our reality. If we make the most use of what we have by practicing gratitude, we will find that all our wants and desires will be satisfied beyond all comprehension. Decrease the number of wants in your life, and you will find abundance.

We have to see through the pain to find the truth. Setting our sights on being grateful helps us to stop seeing through the lens of pain, thus stopping the victim mentality. Having the victim mindset is the most proven way to stay unhappy.

Keeping the company of those who are addicted to the victim mentality is the surest way to cloud our vision and keep us in a state of unhappiness. So, I made amends with my inner child. I reassured him he was safe. I hugged my inner child. I saw memories of my brothers and sisters back home. I was always angry at home. But after seeing through the pain, I once again found the beauty of the home I came from.

I was taught that life was always meant to be hard. I was also blessed to live in a majestic, holy, and fantastical place. Only now do I see why home was such a blessing, though my time there is done. I have to move like I did when I moved out West.

I saw many doors, asking which one I needed to step through. I was told that any door would do, so I stepped through one and into a short cave with a light at the end. I eventually reached the light and then through it. Then, I went to the universe, where I marveled at creation.

trip 5

As the fifth trip started, I asked myself, *What have you been doing this time?* Over the past year, I had focused on graduating from college and looking for somewhere to move. I was shown myself and what I was doing with my life. That feeling of having my life taken from me was explained by how I had been putting too much time into other people's lives.

Subconsciously, I was hoping my life would magically be given purpose the more I stayed attached to other people. I wasn't following my path: I was following the path of others. This ended up making me an NPC.

NPCs in video games are known as Non-Player Characters. They are there to assist with the story but largely do not help drive it forward. The main character drives it forward.

I am the main character of my story, and I was not driving my story forward at all. I was stagnant and living inside my head, hoping some unknown force would bring me a "call to action." The truth I was given was that we always choose to answer our call to action or sit idle while our soul gets bored and we feel as though a Djinn is drinking our life force until it's completely gone.

TAKE
ACTION

The call to action of which I speak is the passions, hobbies, and talents we know we should be pursuing but somewhat put off for many reasons. Doing so takes us off our path as we relinquish control and start following the paths of others. Of course, we lose ourselves in this process. This is easy to do in today's world due to all the stimulation we are surrounded with.

Joseph Campbell coined the term "call to action" in his book *The Hero with a Thousand Faces.* I strongly recommend this to anyone who wants to explore a beautiful mix of psychology and mythos.

I had to keep asking myself what brought all of this on. The answer came to me when I took my dog outside and looked at the mountains in the morning. I noticed the clouds fading above them after days of snow hitting our area hard. I realized how beautiful those were, and in that moment.

I also learned how I have not been paying attention to the many other beautiful things in my life. I was focusing on what was making me unhappy, and by doing so, I was creating a habit of focusing less on what was beautiful each day. This leads us to melancholy and, eventually, infinite sadness, as the Smashing Pumpkins would say.

Once you start on your own path, it will be lonely because it differs from how you have lived. But if you stay true to yourself and maintain course, the right people, the good people who will love you for you, will find you and join you on your journey. So always keep walking forward with your head held high.

And make use of my time. I will write the books I need to write and will dispel the addictions I still struggle with. I will eliminate a large amount of debt and fall in love.

- STAY -
POSITIVE

outro

Recap of Improvements

Lessons from the Final Trip

This last trip was calm. It was like a recap of previous lessons, reminding me to go forward with gratitude. Understand that pain is at the basis of anger, and there is no shortage of anger in a world of pain. When we focus on what we already have that is good, those things become more part of our reality.

When we do this, we stop focusing on our wants: those material things that cost us time that we can never get back.

By doing so, you will cultivate the company of a grateful mindset. Thus, it reduces anxiety and keeps us happy in the present moment of our day-to-day lives.

TIPS FOR A GOOD SESSION &
UPDATE TWO YEARS
LATER TO THE DAY

Since the last session in February of 2022, I was able to do the following:

- *Stopped* 7 out of 9 addictions, sugar being one of the addictions that remain.
- *Started* a luxury loose-leaf tea company, Trenchmen Teas, and build the company as a passion, not look at it as something competitive or a job.
- *Found* a fantastic woman and had the best relationship in my life for over a year. Relationships are not about you. They never are.
- *Climbed* out of debt by focusing

more on the small day-to-day transactions and how impulse buying ruined my life.

- *Finished* this book, my fourth one to date.
- *Healed* from my past.
- *Fixed* the problem of feeling like I was not enough.
- *Healed* the relationship with my father (I am most proud of this).
- *Learned* to set and reinforce healthy boundaries, being firm on what behaviors are unacceptable to tolerate.
- *Wake* up daily with a purpose.
- *Became* much slower to anger and forgive others quicker, realizing that people are not born bad. They are just dealing with their own shit, and I don't need to add shit to their shit sandwich.

And finally, I learned to trust God and do my best to renew this vow daily.

It is important to mentally and physically prepare yourself before taking ketamine if you want to have a positive experience. I will disclose what I did before each session and how I concluded why it is important to follow this guidance.

1. Four hours prior, you need to stop consuming food.

2. Ninety minutes prior, you should stop drinking any liquids because you don't want your session interrupted because you need to use the restroom.

3. A day or two before your session, you must set clear intentions on what you want to discover about yourself. The trick here is to have an idea of a problem or a question you want answered.

4. When you are administered your dose, you should use these intentions

to subtly guide your thoughts while you are under. If you simply let your mind float free, you will find it hard to concentrate on anything and only focus on the physical effects.

5. Ensure that you will not be disturbed during your session and that your sitter is fully aware of the timeline during your journey. I can't stress enough the importance of a good sitter during this time. They will be responsible for helping to eliminate distractions such as pets and anyone who may knock on your door unexpectedly. They will also be keeping time for you. For those who take the pill form known as a trouche, you have to hold the tablet in your cheek or under your tongue for seven minutes before spitting out the remains. From there, they will reset the timer for fifty minutes, the duration of a typical ketamine trip.

6. I found a diffuser very helpful and highly recommend Dragon's Blood, if you can get your hands on some. I

recommend it because it dramatically helps induce a hypnotic state.

7. Ensure you have some eye covering to eliminate the sense of sight during this time.

8. Earbuds or AirPods are also strongly recommended, and a one-hour playlist has binaural beats. But ensure that the music you are listening to is pure. Many artists add background effects or subtle additions that distort the true sounds. The binaural beats I listened to helped guide my emotions and profoundly affected the experience. It is also wise to wear loose, comfortable clothing during your trip. Find a good blanket and pillow to use as well.

You might be asking how I came to find all of this out. When you go through ketamine therapy, you typically will go through four to six sessions. I went through a company called Mindbloom, which provides six sessions' worth of the experience.

During my second session, the sitter I had was very distracted with several things, which caused me to lose focus during my trip. The setting could have been better, too, as we were rushed for time. I woke up early by fifteen minutes during my second session and left the bedroom to find out my sitter was outside on the phone. The sitter should be nearby and should check on the person under about once every ten to fifteen minutes. This ensures that the person under is not trying to get out of bed or move around or anything during their trip.

Finally, I encourage everyone not to fear facing your inner demons. Once you face something, you shine a light on it. The light takes the power away from the darkness, even the darkest parts within yourself. So, go boldly forward and seek healing. And with that, I wish everyone the best of luck and the greatest of peace.

About the Author

Longstanding resident of Santa Claus, Indiana, Anthony Farina is the author of the YA novel *ForeverVerse,* the setting of which is based upon the grounds of St. Meinrad Monastery where Anthony played as a child. Anthony is also author of *Angels in Sadr City: The Final Fight for Baghdad* (2009/2015), a memoir of his experience as a combat soldier in the definitive Battle of Sadr City.

ForeverVerse
A Fairy Tale
WRITTEN BY ANTHONY FARINA
ILLUSTRATED BY JACKIE NICKEL
Available on Amazon

Available on Amazon

Mindbloom

Ketamine Therapy

www.mindbloom.com

Traitmarker Media, LLC
www.traitmarkermedia.com